NAMING THE DEAD

Robert Collins

FutureCycle Press

Mineral Bluff, Georgia

Published by FutureCycle Press
Mineral Bluff, Georgia, USA

ISBN 978-0-9839985-7-0

For Laurie, always there

Contents

V.

VI.

VII.

"Now let us go
into the blind world waiting here below . . ."

—Dante, *The Inferno*

I.

Those Who Have Vanished

We read of them in the papers
in notices smaller than obituaries.
They're the strangers who step out
one evening for a brief breath of air
or to the store to pick up some bread
and, turning a corner or leaving
the train, vanish and never return.

The police put out their APB's,
but somehow they slip through
like aliens swimming under water.
Search lights sweep the suburbs
like the second hands of clocks,
and the river's dragged for bodies,
but dragnets fill only with shadows.

I think of those I've loved
and thought I knew and lost.
How we got so far apart
we couldn't find a way back
remains a mystery to me
as if we left nothing behind
we could ever have wanted.

And sometimes, like tonight, I think
that someone lost like myself
might be out there searching still,
dragging the long, slow waters
of moonless nights without sleep,

and I want to say, "I'm still here,
not far away, I haven't forgotten,"
as we each fade farther and farther
into the lives we have chosen.

II.

Enuresis

At least I never embarrassed my parents
at school the way that Kathy Rumph did—
a small puddle of sour urine pooling
under her desk while she tried to pretend
nothing too peculiar was occurring.
I reserved my episodes for nighttime
when my lack of self-control couldn't be
so easily detected and shame could be
delayed until tomorrow.
                              Toward dawn
I'd wake up damp and cold, aware
I'd gone and done it one more time,
the insides of my tender thighs chapped
from steeping half the night in my own
juices. Mom and Dad tried everything
to cure me—repeated trips to specialists
for further diagnoses, more exercise,
imipramine, hypnosis, and rubber sheets
to sleep on. They even frightened me
with tales of boys my age in Africa
whose parents tethered poison toads
to the inside of their thighs to startle them
if they began to pee. Despite Mom's
and Dad's misgivings and one doctor's
reassurance that it was just a phase
I'd soon grow out of, they scowled at me
in silence every morning as if I could
control my bladder and wet the bed
deliberately to spite them.
                              Perhaps I just

slept soundly as a child or had a tiny bladder
that failed to alert my fouled-up amygdala
at the crucial moment or I just never dreamed
of water and didn't secrete anti-diuretic hormone.
But maybe it was something more disturbing
and deeper, as the psychiatrist they consulted
had maintained—lesions like sunspots flaring
in my brain, disrupting all communication,
which would soon put an end to wetting
the bed and let the night terrors begin.

Invisible Runner

That house is standing in the vacant lot
on the corner where I used to cross
home plate, and I can't begin to count
all the times I tried to drive myself in.
As I cruise by now, I see strangers inside
eating supper where the infield was,
leaning toward their plates in candlelight
where once I snagged hot liners leaping
off the bats of boys on summer mornings,
foul or fair. Years later when the family
tells this story, we always say how odd
it was that no one built a house there
till the day we finally moved away.

Tonight, I spy the current owners
gesturing over dinner and chatting idly
where I flashed signs to invisible men
and gauged the depth of long fly balls.
Then I remember the day I died
with the winning run hugging second
and ran away and wouldn't come back
all night until the van was loaded.
I realize then what my life is like
as I inch off in the darkness, looking
back over my shoulder, invisible
in my old haunts, trying to steal home,
with everything still in the balance.

Polio

All that summer
polio broke out like brush fire
young boys can't stamp out
and run away from.

In the middle of the night,
we'd wake to sirens,
the red light of the ambulance
pumping outside for hours,

making us cower deeper
into the shadows of our rooms.
One boy disappeared
into a body gone rigid,

the iron lung a bathysphere around him.
Only his eyes grown large showed
how much he feared the long descent,
his odd still dreams filled

with strange mutations of the deep:
pteropod, frill shark, jellyfish medusa.
The rest of us, the lucky ones,
grew afraid of one another,

flexed and felt our muscles,
and at the slightest ache
imagined our own descent,
the crackle of shrimp in our ears

like sparks
sizzling on the rooftops of our houses.

The Blue Flames

Like the name emblazoned across the backs
of our indigo jerseys, we burned cool and gaseous—
clumsiest ball club in the county, clad in dungarees
and sneakers, no challenge for the Fireballs,
our cocky cross-town rivals, who took the field
by storm as if they owned it, dazzling in crimson
pinstripes, polished cleats, and red caps stitched
with sculpted lightning, bleached and creased
as any barnstorming nine of the old Negro circuit.

We hailed from the other side of town—losers
who feared the first cut every time we tried to make
the more exclusive squad because we couldn't throw
or hit or catch in the glare of a coach's withering gaze.
After every put-out, they whipped the ball around
the infield, gaining an advantage before another pitch
was thrown. We muffed lazy pop-ups, pegged
relays into the dirt, and booted easy grounders
even in practice while the Fireballs stayed patient,

certain to fatten their stats at our expense—a breather
on any team's schedule sweeter than winning by forfeit.
They sent sentinels to stand at first and third and wave
on the circling queue of runners they anticipated having.
We sat the bench and laughed about blowing signs
and going 0 for August. Between innings, Harry Barry,
backstop and spiritual leader on and off the field, took
his glass eye out (where he'd just misjudged another pop-
up) and smoked unfiltered Luckies behind the bleachers.

They took the field determined while we strolled
out to our positions, pinching unfinished Winstons,
expecting to fall behind and be routed early. Hence,
it came as no surprise when another summer ignored
the paltry backfires we'd lit as a diversion, hoping
to cool off our opponents and ease the pain of losing,
acting like we couldn't have cared less, leapt the fire
wall we'd erected between July and August, dreaming
of vacation when the season ended, and burned on.

The Jump Shot

for Walt Meyer

That summer you taught me the jump shot,
shadows stretched to bat back my attempts.
Over and over I spun balls arcing at the rim,
trying to do exactly what you showed me.
Those moments when I got it right,
time resumed between rising and falling
only with the soft twang of the goal,
the dry hiss of the net, and the unheard cheers
of thousands I invented to keep going.

Sometimes now, at the peak of my jump,
we are on the playground once again,
and I don't even have to look toward you
to know the shot I'm taking's going in.
For a moment I hang weightless, almost happy,
though I know when I come down
you won't be there to approve,
and I will have to fall back and defend.

Overpass

Some teenage boy in town must have gone to
any length to publicize his horniness and longing,
hanging upside down in darkness to scrawl
Jennifer Loves Jason Forever, probably getting
it backwards, hoping to assure her love would last
as long as he was certain his would by sealing it in
words on the concrete abutment of the freeway
overpass I've just driven under, his best friend
Bubba cursing and grabbing him desperately
by the legs until the county magistrate arrived.

All three reside in the small town several miles
beyond the beltway stenciled on the exit sign,
which might as well be the far side of the moon
as far as contact with the outside world's concerned.
There football reigns on Friday night in autumn,
and veterans of foreign occupations promenade
their Purple Hearts in the Memorial Day Parade.
His face greasy and enflamed as a dropped pizza,
the boy teeters forever on the brink of flunking
out of high school and races his rusty red Camaro

down forlorn county roads, crazed by boredom
and hormones, biding his time till a mechanic's
job opens up at the local garage. The girl itches
to be knocked up ASAP with the first of many kids
whose given names will all begin with the letter "J"
as though they're hamsters or gerbils, hardly 17
and her figure gone to fat already. Leaving behind
the overpass, I know the fate of Jennifer and Jason

is sealed already too. They're divorced or living
with their parents, trailing an expanding brood

of whimpering dependents through the aisles
of the nearby K-Mart every other weekend,
love lost somewhere during sleepless nights
in endless quarrels over formula and diapers.
I know I never hung suspended in the dark,
giddy with adrenaline and danger, head-over-
heels to proclaim, however foolishly, my love.
More than half my life ago, a terrified teenager
like Jason, I believed such feats of ingenuity
and daring as scrawling my name or any words

I'd written in improbable places might guarantee
that love would last forever. I had to win the girl
who wore my high school ring wrapped in red angora
the fattest panda at the county fair by knocking
over bottles, tossing rings, or sinking free throws.
But we failed to stay together long enough to see
how fragile love can be, spared the bitter words
uttered in the heat of anger within hearing of the kids
we surely would have had, which banish love forever,
while nothing anyone can say will make it last.

Junior Lifesaving

What were all those lessons for,
up to my neck in brackish water
behind the crumbling cabanas,
learning to breathe and crawl,
treading the dank lagoon at 8:00 a.m.,
perfecting the dead man's float?
I wanted to be back on shore
flirting with the girls out early
to tan in their trim bikinis
or training to swim faster and farther
for gold or learning to dive,
soaring and arcing forward with ease,
in flight all eyes upon me,
before parting our pool's
clear water with hardly a splash.

Later, barely holding my own
against swirling currents,
I couldn't even save myself.
I was the one needing rescue,
gasping and flailing, crying for help
even in shallow water—
whose strength gave out,
whose courage failed first,
who never held another in my arms,
risking the saving embrace
that could drag us under,
or learned to love despite that shadow
we glimpse in open water,
its black fin turning toward us,
rising to drag us down.

Catch

for my father

Sometime after supper
during my annual summer visit,
one of us uncovers
our battered Rawlings baseball gloves,
"the finest in the field,"
at the bottom of the foyer closet,
and we head out to the backyard,
lobbing a shredded Spalding back and forth,
squatting and spitting
and shaking our legs to unlimber,
wind-milling the stiffness
out of our arms between tosses
like aging relievers who can't remember
the last time they were summoned
with the game on the line.

Despite years of beer and cigarettes,
at some point you always declare
there's nothing I can throw at you
that you won't be able to handle.
As dusk descends we rear back farther,
smiles fading from our faces,
and uncork heaters low and hard,
scuffed cowhide exploding into leather,
to see who'll be the first to flinch.

The old anger at how we've failed
again and again in the clutch
to be what the other wanted surfaces

unspoken like the love between us,
each of your pitches cutting
imaginary corners finer and finer
till I sense how frightened you are
of all you might be forced to feel
should you ever lose your control.

Surprised and baffled one more time
by the flutter of your knuckler,
I bobble the ball and drop it.
My glove hand still stinging
from all those fast balls,
I turn away and curse you,
curse this game of saying nothing
neither one of us can win,
wind up and fling the ball back,
the curve you wouldn't teach me
to throw breaking in the dirt,
bouncing past you into the dark.

III.

28 NAMING THE DEAD

The Lone Survivor

He's the one who finally returns
from the wreckage, speechless, dragging
his shattered torso along, to confirm
the worst has happened already.

Those waiting on the ground for word
of next of kin wring their hands and weep.
Secretly, they despise him. They need
to know why he was spared, not trapped

in the fatal crash forever like the rest.
After baffled surgeons bandage
his unblinking eyes, he tries to describe
the eerie quiet at the site of the disaster,

but he can't remember what broke down
or comprehend why he was saved
against all odds, miraculously thrown clear
of the carnage at the critical moment.

Nor can he proffer words of comfort
to the living—that the others didn't suffer
in the fire—their screams erupting,
the fuselage exploding in his dreams.

He can't explain why he's the one
who noted something major had gone wrong
hours back before the flight had veered
off-course, its stuttering engines on fire.

Day after day he tells the same story
till even CNN grows tired of his lying

while those beside themselves with grief
agree the accident could not occur

exactly the way he's described it.
Surely he deserves some blame
for the disaster though maimed for life
himself, burned beyond recognition.

Escape

For months you have it planned.
You cut your vocal chords for safety.
You are freed from the bracelets of sound.
You rub your body down
with clay and charcoal
and go past the guard.
He is sleeping.
You go over the fence.
It is easy.
Fog. You see fog.
You think you hear dogs.
You swim a river,
climb a mountain,
and walk through torrid jungle
until you reach a swamp
where a woman is waiting
with money, a boat, and clothes.
When you arrive,
she is smoking a cigarette
and fondling her breasts in the moonlight.
You boil your old clothes and eat them.
After a day or two,
she is pecked by a bulbous green insect
and dies of malaria
just as you had planned.
When you reach the city,
you are exhausted, dirty, and starving,
but you've done it. Escaped.
You are free.
You assume a new face, a new name,

begin a new life.
When you hear the authorities
have never discovered your absence,
you are overjoyed.
You begin to devise an even better plan.
This one must be perfect.
It must get you back in.

The Magician's Assistant

Cold in the skimpy costume
the magician insisted I wear,
I confess I was a little afraid
though no one in the audience
seemed apprehensive or sad,
certain as they must have been
that it was all an illusion
and he'd surely bring me back.

Sealed inside the magic box,
I searched for secret passages,
hollow bottoms, trap doors,
chutes that might slide open,
leading to a room backstage
where I would soon be spirited
until he gave the signal to return.

Before I had a chance to panic,
my flesh began to tingle, atoms
to accelerate and spin, molecules
to split and rearrange themselves,
instantly enlarging the emptiness
I'd only vaguely sensed before.

As I hovered invisible overhead,
I watched as he broke the coffin
open, heard the astonished crowd
wildly applauding the emptiness,
amazed myself that we'd pulled
it off without a dress rehearsal.

Never had I felt so much alone.
For the first time in my life,
I saw through all the illusions
I concocted to survive—believing
there could be no magic without me.

After a thousand nights like this,
I would prefer to be dismembered,
sawed in half, or hypnotized, squatting
on all fours, quacking or barking,
making an utter fool of myself on stage
in front of total strangers—

                anything
to escape the bottomless black pit
I tumble into every time we do this
trick and I feel like cutting my throat
or slashing my wrists, unable
to live or die without illusions.

Extras

The entire cast dead already,
somehow resurrected they appear,
quietly breaking the surface
of old black and white movies
or stepping out of the shadows
for the briefest of scenes
in Saturday's second feature
to deliver a package, whisper
a message in someone's ear,
utter a line or two, and vanish
from the silver screen forever.

Never actually touching
the stars, they're the extras
who fail to make it,
never playing the leading men,
matinee idols who get the girl—
giving voice to their passion
while locked in the fleshy embrace
of some sultry femme fatale—
or die valiantly trying,
sending her back to her spouse.

We'll never know what
hidden dreams they cherished
or how slowly they began to see
how their dreams failed them,
suffering alone for years
off screen before surrendering
to whiskey or the river.

They are the unknowns
who swam a long way up
from the bottom to get here
and, barely breaking the surface,
were dragged back down in an instant,
the lines that might have saved
them, let them cry for help,
as yet unwritten,
their whole lives passing
before our eyes.

The Editor of Dreams

She works all night
while the darkness flickers,
clipping and splicing each frame
before passing the reels
to the sleepy projectionist.

Sometimes she includes bad takes
you don't remember shooting.
Out of control you're falling
from a hundred stories up,
a stunned, unhappy double.

Or you come to being chased
down half-deserted city streets,
a scream stuck in your throat.
Or you wake up one day paralyzed,
water already seeping under the door.

She always censors the sex scenes,
rousing you abruptly
at the very moment of sweetness,
leaving you alone and forlorn
inside the dark theater.

Near dawn she yawns and stretches
and gets ready to head home,
the screen blank, the marquee dark,
the ticket window shuttered.
She boards the last express

before it turns into the shadows
and the lower side of town.
Spools of over-exposures
you're not yet ready to view
unfurl on the cutting-room floor.

Prince Frog

Having changed two times already
from polliwog to tadpole,
from tadpole into frog,
warily I waited in the bog,
ill-at-ease, isolate, agog with possibilities,
for something more to happen.

Submerged at night I dreamed
a comely woman found me where I
wallowed in the swamp, found me indeed
repulsive, yet took me in her palm
and changed me with a kiss
happily ever after into a handsome prince.

But however fast I crooned myself
to sleep, the magic always vanished
and I awoke dispelled, warts and rheumy eyes
and tacky skin, stuck back here in the mire,
scepterless, bewildered and alone,
my queen, my crown, my fiefdom gone.

No longer do I dream the ardent kiss
of any princess, however sweet or deep,
can possibly transform me. Wide awake,
I squat, listening as my nemeses approach,
whispering sly conspiracies as they stride
inexorably toward me from below.

However brief, however ill-advised,
I reign, croaking and content, heirless

suzerain of a dank, diminished realm.
Because of what I am and where I've been,
I should know, if any creature can,
lasting change comes only from within.

The Scream

(after a lithograph by Edvard Munch, 1895)

In the foreground I am,
water on the brain,
each lead-deaf ear
shot clean away,
incapable of hearing.

My gaunt and fishy hands read
throats, become my interlocutors
as I wail in a language
of sign deprived of sound.

Once I was a peasant
within the simmering fens.
A woman said she loved me
and lived with another man.

Deftly, she kissed
my sagging lobes and twisted eyes.
They hissed like anvils and flew off dumbly,
lost in the whistling dark.

Now screaming
but without a sound,
I am disembodied,
ghost of the living,
aching to contact the dead.

Two days journey back,
I crossed dead water
sickening some cows.

The two dark men on the road
over my right shoulder
observe and follow at a distance,
careful not to come too close.

The road ahead,
out of the picture, goes on,
goes down forever.

They are all behind me—
poison, darkness, ambush, drowning,
every means of dying,
all out of ear-shot, unheard of.

The Counterfeiter's Confession

Hidden in dingy cellars,
I learned to etch the plates,
choose the finest grades of paper,
and sample the inks,
always a step ahead of the police.

One winter I heard of people starving
in the streets of the Great Republic
and jumping out of windows,
but I couldn't distinguish
the true from the false.

For a very long time,
all the money I made
was so obviously unreal
and of no value whatsoever—
the faces of famous statesmen
oddly averted or erased—
I couldn't even give it away.

Then I had major problems
I was never able to solve
with all the larger denominations.

After that last fiasco
and one more major depression,
I decided to go it alone,
to make my own money
whatever the cost,
no more imitations,
though I knew I invited arrest
and hours of inquisition.

Left to my own resources,
more grateful than I've ever been,
I go on inking and stamping
huge sheets of uncut paper
of value to no one but me,
bold colors and odd denominations
I'll never be able to spend,
every bit of it worthless,
money to burn.

Always Stay Calm. Never Shout Fire.

It happens unexpectedly
one evening over drinks

while the guests are climbing
the ladders of conversation,

smoke gathering over their heads,
a wisp of nets,

the parlor getting brighter and brighter.
When the sofa bursts into flames,

the flowers in the carpet
flinging petals of fire,

you want to cry out
but can only manage a whisper

while the woman perspiring
in the overstuffed chair,

her tongue a glowing coal,
asks for a little more ice.

You try to edge toward the door,
sirens pinwheeling just beneath

the icecaps in your blood,
but already the hinges are squealing,

the doorknob sizzling,
and still the others don't notice.

They drift from room to room,
their cocktails beginning to boil,

parts already aflame.
You raise a window and wait,

calm, not shouting fire,
for the door only fire can open.

IV.

48   NAMING THE DEAD

Stroke

for my grandmother Veronica Martin (1894-1976)

You lie there slumped,
and I can hardly bear to look—
half of you caved in,
the rotten beams shoring up
the long tunnel
collapsing under your flesh,
a word almost forming on your lips
like a faint tapping
through sixty feet of coal.

You see but cannot read
the flowered cards propped
like Day-Glo churches by your bed;
and hear but cannot comprehend
the gasping tubes and beeping dials
drilling for your vital signs.
All the rest could go at any moment,
yet you still don't know I'm here
like that night eighteen years ago
when I woke in the avalanching dark
and heard you weeping the name
of your husband dead a year.
Even then, across that muffled rubble,
I couldn't reach you.

More than once since then,
I've wondered how your life would end,
but every time I've turned from it,
a stone I couldn't budge.

I stand now, your hand in mine,
powerless to pull you back
from the darkness on that side,
unable to let go, calling out,
not your name, but my own.

Neverlost

for Brian Conley (1947-2002)

I.

Sinking swiftly in the last sick bed
you swear you've made yourself
thanks to forty years of booze and drugs,
you're dying of pancreatic cancer.
Jimmy Q. and I career across Boston
in the Volvo wagon he's rented,
trying to get to see you one more time.
Fully fitted with the fanciest new options,
our ride includes the latest GPS,
which shows us where we want to go
and the easiest way to get there,
so we'll never be lost again.

Yet we keep missing our turns,
prompting the patient female voice
that guides us to pause and reconstruct
the route, speeding us farther and farther
from the shadows waiting at your house.
Cursing the computer and the Big Dig,
over-budget and still under construction,
we begin to wonder if earth has been
surveyed and charted so precisely
that harried, frustrated travelers like us
can be directed invisibly from above—
a notion you scoffed at in college
unless it was the government, not god.

When we were young and free and certain
we could change the world, we knew we'd
never live in quiet desperation, everything
we believed in weighed and measured, nights
deprived of mystery. But we mellowed, made
concessions to survive and find ourselves,
and nearly drank all faith in miracles away.
Now, none of us can say how we've reached
this impasse—all the laughter, love that didn't
last, hashish schemes, poems we wrote and bad
hangovers, songs that sang equality and peace
reduced to one, abrupt, unanticipated turn
you can't keep yourself from taking.

II.

Outside in the shriveled garden
you planted six months earlier in spring
just before your final diagnosis,
we talk of taking one more ride together
as if we might recapture better days
and laugh again for a little while at least,
but pills and nurse's protocols prevail,
and we sit in forlorn silence mostly
as daylight sifts swiftly away.

What's left that we haven't said
already or tried to write to one another
through the years? Desperate to keep
the conversation going, I say your name
too loud too many times and startle
your eyes open, asking empty questions

as if the words we've trusted all our lives
might hold you here a little longer.
You prove the better guide as always,
uttering the one word we've been trying
not to say when we aren't even sure
you're listening to our silly conversation
about what the future holds and stupidly
I ask, "Who knows where life might lead?"

We should've picked you up, put
you in the car in your drab pajamas,
and gone for one more drive. Maybe
if we'd described our destination
in more detail or entered better data
or abandoned altogether any notion of arriving,
we might have found the one way out,
speeding beyond our doubts and hesitation
to the route that could have saved you.
Despite the claims of science and religion,
none of us knew what to say or where to turn.
We're lost the whole damn weekend.

Naming the Dead

for Rae Jeanne Carr (1949-2009)

We gather on the mall at dusk
in front of Alter Hall, the classroom
windows icy blanks behind us,
Kent State still several months away.

We've pledged to stay all night,
however long it takes till graying men
who strut the corridors of power
hear our pleas and end the war.

Red-faced, sputtering with rage,
we wade a shallow pool of luminescence
the lone security light provides,
which only makes the night air colder,

and begin to read as we've been taught
in alphabetical order—the metal clamp
for running up Old Glory gonging
the naked flagpole wildly in the wind

like a church bell tolling out of time
as if uttering the names of total strangers
in any order might bring peace
and resurrect the dead.

We're young and still believe that words
can change the world, having no idea how
long the list is, longer than this darkness,
how many more are dying as we read,

or how much time will pass,
how many more recited
before we hear our own names
read out loud.

Poem for Vicki

The night we met in 1969
through a haze of dope and booze,
you talked about your life
and laughed almost till dawn,
recounting all that had gone wrong—
your parents dead, your husband gone,
and men you hardly knew
rattling your windows at all hours.

As you spoke, your pain arced
toward me like sparks from a wire
ripped down by the wind.
I was afraid if somehow I grasped it,
I'd never be able to let go.
I got so drunk that later in the dark,
as we were making love, I could not
remember what you looked like.

Years later learning of your death,
I hear your laugh and see your face again
rising in the haze of summer twilight,
knowing now there's no escape from pain
and I'll die if I ever let go, knowing
I'll never know you as I could have—
completely out of my mind at last, plunging
in darkness, beside myself with joy.

Always There

for Denny Chambers (1951-2001)

Back in the day we drank till
dawn, playing jazz and laughing

at the brash, impromptu diatribe
on trash-can lids and rat control

I'd delivered in my delirium
at the campus bar we haunted

and how the band you played the bass
in had begun to call you Draino.

Today, I heard that wordless tune
you turned me on to—"Always There"

by Ronnie Laws—and one night
played over and over till daylight

and your tired wife, rising to get
dressed for work, assailed us,

blaming me as usual for all the sleep
she'd lost since I always seemed

to be there as you drank your life
away. I still think of you and her

and those lost, besotted interludes
every time I hear it. Were we moved

by the plaintive ache of the tenor sax,
how it seemed to insist some bonds

must never break no matter how
much time or distance intervenes?

The last time we got drunk together
twenty years before, inhaling Harp

in that Sinn Fein bar in downtown
San Francisco, we never dreamed

that anything would change
while furtive tables on all sides

plotted revolution. I was a year
away from being sober. Soon

you'd be too drunk to keep a job.
Drinking through the afternoon

as the fog off the sea descended
and the light sifted slowly away,

we didn't think about the future.
We only wanted to be certain

another round was on its way
and we had cash enough to pay.

No friend or fortune-teller
could convince us to believe

in a decade you'd be gone, hung
with your own hand on Xmas Eve,

having no one left to call
and nothing left to live for,

leaving me befuddled, wondering
what had happened, how you,

how anybody ends up so alone,
asking why I wasn't there.

Casualty

for Carol Shelley

When I heard you'd set yourself on fire,
trying to destroy the lovely body you depended
on so much and then began to loathe
more than the men who craved to embrace it,
and lay alone for weeks in ICU burned
past recognition, I was horrified, remembering
I'd betrayed you, unable to forget
that snowy evening half our lives ago
when we ended up at your place
after all the bars had closed.

To persuade you to remove your clothes,
I whispered empty promises I didn't mean
to keep, sure we'd never meet again.
By then you were a walking victim
of the 60's, in and out of psych wards,
diagnosed psychotic, suicidal, clinically
depressed because you'd smoked
a ton of reefer, swallowed too much LSD,
and let yourself believe the shameless lies
of far too many men who wouldn't even kiss
you in the morning when they left.

I told you I'd be different, but I might
as well have helped you strike the match
because I didn't hear your anger or sense
how you'd begun to smolder years before,
posing naked for classes at the college

so you wouldn't have to waitress to pay
your way through school. At first you felt
uptight and nervous when smirking students
ogled you; any girl who took her clothes off
in a classroom must be easy or so some seemed
to think.
        Soon it was a job like any other,
your torso just a model to be copied—
ample breasts, narrow hips, and supple thighs—
like a bowl of waxy fruit or a vase of artificial
flowers—most students hardly conscious
you were naked until you disappeared,
no longer present most days even to yourself,
but you didn't plan on posing nude forever.
You held on to your dream that come
the revolution, power would revert to
the people and everything you needed
be provided by the state.
                      Confused,
used up at thirty, you only wanted what
we all want—someone who would see you
for who you really are and love you for yourself.
Too late to ask forgiveness, I realize when
you lit the match, you'd gone profoundly crazy
like the inscrutable Buddhist holy men
we watched go up in flames on the nightly news
in protest, sacrificing everything for love.

New Year's Day: Red River Gorge, 1973

for Ford Swetnam (1938-2002)

We woke restive with the waxing light,
first ones up and about that New Year,
or so I liked to think—not high, hung-over,
or drunk, first time (for me at least) in weeks.
The day before when we reached the park,
you glanced at me and grinned, wide-eyed,
shouting in your shrill, barbaric yawp,
"I said Wild Turkey, not cold turkey!"
deftly turning a phrase when we couldn't
buy a bottle anywhere in eastern Kentucky.
Then we hit the trailhead to hike our pain
away and try to outdistance our sorrow,
both of us stumbling badly at love again.
I fell in behind, fearing you'd find out
how frightened I was of anything feral.

Years later we hiked the Blue Ridge
in late winter, walking the trail you helped
construct. Despite warning signs posted
on the door of every privy and scat steaming
at our feet, you kindly reassured me the last
brown bear had been sighted in Virginia
years before. Spooked, I shadowed your
footsteps, following your lead as always,
but lost you in the haze ahead and began
to panic as daylight drained and the air
grew colder. Then, I turned a bend where
you waited with a fire already banked,

a hearty supper simmering, and the gift
of your friendship, laughter, and wit.
Now, you've vanished again, blazing

the way into wilderness where I'm still
too frightened to venture alone as you
had in that final collection of poems
you sent me, work I felt wholly your own—
lanky, laconic, quirky, and lithe—though
I never wrote and told you. Ford, friend
who taught me so much about failure,
we never got that gulp of Wild Turkey
together, and I never got to say so long.
Somewhere up the narrow trail ahead,
I'll top a rise perhaps or round a bend
and find you lolling beside a burgeoning fire,
though it's late and the light is fading fast,
waiting patiently to assure me one more time
that the going really hasn't been so bad.

Via Sacra

for Dick Hague and Jim Quinlivan

One steamy morning in June,
we climb an Indian mound in Marietta
where Adenas buried their dead
and kept a mile-long swath
cut clear to the river.
We move without a sound into the shade
among the fading ghosts
piled under the hillside,
darkness looming nearer,
as if wondering why we've paused
to pay our last respects
before taking to the river.
Later, on the water,
making for the other shore,
a black barge heaped with coal
about to plow us under,
we find how we've misjudged
the hurl and sweep of currents,
how far across it is,
how hard we've yet to paddle,
haze shimmering mute ghosts
above unsettling wake.

Near dusk we pause
for one last look at the Ohio,
currents we surrendered to
and surfaced from confounded,
before hoisting our canoe

and heading out, upland,
where rising waters never reach,
toward dead-end jobs,
lost love, untold deaths to come,
lives that keep us striving.
We spend half the night ashore,
singing, laughing, swapping stories,
anything to keep ourselves awake;
and then we lie exhausted,
dreaming of the river,
drifting in and out
on sleep's slow currents,
amazed at how the faceless dead
arise on summer nights
and stroll down to dark water
chanting praises in strange tongues
to bathe their wounds
and wash their pain away.

V.

Going Home

for my brother Ed

Leaving Killarney behind, we cruise around
County Kerry for hours, seeking the tiny hamlet
Jeremiah Flynn was born in—expert horseman
and sire of our Irish clan, burned in a stable fire
on Staten Island a century or more before,
back across the ocean he'd sailed over.

When we locate the crossroads of Bally Finnane,
the only unlocked door in any of the buildings
(and there aren't very many) lunges open stiffly
into the foyer of the pub we knew would be here
if we know one another and our family history
at all. It isn't much of a pub to speak of really—

besides the well-stocked shelves of liquor—
a few rickety tables and chairs and a wooden counter
where spirits are bought with euros, not punts;
more a flimsy excuse for having a pint with the lads—
not that either of us dreamed a hero's welcome
or anything resembling the prodigal's return.

*Faith and begorra, here's two of Jeremiah's
boys come back from America at last and both
of them successful—the younger one a lawyer
and the other a college professor, having made
a name for themselves as we always expected.
Then singing and dancing hours into the night.*

Soon we sense we do want something more
than the few mute, shuttered houses we find

and photograph from every conceivable angle
as though if we take enough pictures the image
of a distant relation might emerge in a window
as they're developed, a smudge on the film—

some identifying sign or shiver of connection
with this town our ancestors sprang from,
not just the broken man we find smoking alone
in the pub—which isn't open for business—
surly, taciturn, red-faced, surely one of our own,
too hung-over or drunk to welcome us home.

The Bar in the Lobby of the Peabody Hotel

One night I tell my closest friends
during dinner if I ever decide to drink
again, I'll begin in the bar in the lobby
of the Peabody Hotel in Memphis
where every day the ducks waddle down
at nine on their way from the roof
and out again at five and I once saw
Stephen Stills stuck in a revolving door,
looking rumpled and hung-over as if
he'd stayed up drinking half the night.
My good friends laugh and roll their eyes.
They don't believe I'll ever do it after
more than fifteen years without a drink,
yet when they inquire why the bar
in the lobby of such a famous old hotel,
I can't find the words to tell them.
I suppose it's connected somehow
with the river, Beale St., and the delta
blues I love, and certainly the distance.
It takes at least four hours to drive
from where I live in central Alabama
up Corridor X to Memphis, ample time
to change my mind and turn around
if I have second thoughts about that drink,
but it's also something more than that,
some strange sensation I can't grasp—
the way the lengthening summer light
floods the hotel windows, immersing
huge upholstered chairs, Persian rugs,
and potted plants, filling me with longing,

while patrons seated at the bar chat softly
between sips from slender champagne flutes
as if the next time might be different,
drinking the way I always dreamed it
could be in such a posh, upscale saloon
where nothing shameful ever happens,
the waning afternoon made endless, ease
and comfort on tap forever. Maybe I'd find
that William James was right—sobriety
says no to life while alcohol embraces it
and death, shouting from the rooftops.
Maybe then, I wouldn't have to suffer,
raising my glass to make a toast, the first
of many, while outside night descends,
in love once more with the spinning world
I've always just wanted to be part of.

Assembling the Brain

for Pat and Jennifer

Cleaning the garage,
I find a cardboard cutout
of the brain my wife and daughter
must have purchased at the mall,
put up, and then forgotten.
I look over the instructions
and, inspired, decide to construct it.
Locked upstairs in the study,
I pore over its folds and insertions
like a mad doctor
about to lift the filched prize
from a jar of formaldehyde,
the open skylight flickering overhead.
All too quickly I discover,
mad or not, I'm no brain surgeon
and not smart enough to complete it.
I can't possibly distinguish
the hippocampus from the thalamus,
the white meat from the dark.
I don't give up, though, till I realize
this brain was probably meant for me
and not merely as a test of my IQ.
I recall how my wife and daughter
have attempted with solicitude and love
to tame this life-long bachelor,
often ornery as Frankenstein,
and make him easier to live with.
I remember how they've humored me,

rolled their eyes and smiled,
when I've sought to give advice,
and the standing joke around our house,
which even I can't honestly deny,
is that I'm the dumbest
despite my three degrees.
Then I suspect they've given up
the subtler tactics they've employed
to try to make me more humane
and these cutouts are a model
of the brain they've been planning
all along to transplant in secret,
so they'll know without looking
exactly where to make incisions
when they come for me in the dark.

Red Giant

to E. O.

Maybe you've met this sort of man before,
just past middle-age, pausing oddly
at the curb as if to ponder a line or turn
of phrase, an image he's constructing,
crimson-faced from years of smoking
Marlboro Reds and gulping cans of Bud—
self-confident and self-propelled
but bloated, overweight and paunchy,
neglecting exercise for decades
except perhaps to mow the lawn,
who seems to have read every good book
ever written and authored several
decent ones himself, a star of more
than average candle power, burning
distinctly if unspectacularly, in a distant
area of sky till one day he suddenly
wheezes and gasps, runs out of gas,
flashes red and swells up larger
while his core implodes with a jolt,
and he becomes a red giant, vaporizing
everything in reach as his center cools
and inner fires bank, who can't believe
it's happening to him, that there's any
power in the cosmos greater than himself,
the lifeless planets orbiting around him,
pulverized, reduced to ashes, torched.

Logging on to Amazon.Com and Finding Out My Book Ranks 2,279,515 in Sales

At first I'm surprised and delighted
to find my book for sale online
alongside Hemingway and Shakespeare
and all the rest of the old masters
who were never wrong about suffering
and knew it firsthand almost as well as I do.
What's more, someone has actually
bought my book—a stranger in a distant
town perhaps, who paid $6.95 to read
and contemplate my poems alone in private.
Scrolling down, I find no one's reviewed
the book yet, and it's not threatening
the best-sellers. For weeks its ranking
stays the same till I begin to wonder
what other unacknowledged works of genius
occupy the slots above and below me,
but I can't seem to find that information.
I console myself with the knowledge
that only other poets read poesy these days,
and even though my book won't sell,
I can still be proudly counted one of
Shelley's unacknowledged senators,
if not of the world, at least of Alabama
though that's a crowd of scoundrels
I'm not eager to be part of. Then I find
the line at the foot of the page, noting
that the reader(s) who bought my book also
purchased titles by other famous writers

like Mary Herczog, distinguished author
of *LA and Disneyland for Dummies,*
Bob Sehlinger, whose works include
Israel Past and Present and *Food in Art,*
Rick Garman, who penned the timeless classic
The Complete Idiot's Travel Guide to Las Vegas
as if being a dummy in Southern California
isn't punishment enough, and Carol Stout,
whose fickle muse helped her produce
The Chick's Guide to Football—
not a Shakespeare or Hemingway among them.
At first I wonder if five different people
might have bought my book but quickly realize
if they had, it would rank much higher.
I'm forced, then, to acknowledge
that my ideal reader, the faceless one
for whom I sweated endless hours working
on those poems, sobbing and losing sleep
and probably ruining my marriage, is more
or less a middle-aged Jewish woman
who likes to look at art and eat and gamble
on football and wants to travel but doesn't
know how. Somehow I'm oddly elated
by that. Though not the audience I imagined
thirty years ago when I first thought I'd try
my hand at writing poems, I'm grateful now
to have one reader, whoever she might be,
who reads poetry for pleasure and is not
a poet, who reads poetry purely for love.

Teaching My Daughter
How to Swim Underwater

I have to lure you to the water,
urge you to submerge your head,
and teach you how to breathe and hold
your breath, which sometimes you threaten
to hold forever, puffing like a blowfish.

You can't get the hang of kicking off,
relaxing your torso enough to accept
its burden and sink to the murky depths below.
All the life in you lifts you to the surface.
I try to tell you not to be afraid, I'm here,

show you how to dive and reach for bottom,
convinced one day, enraptured with the deep,
you'll look back and laugh at how you struggled
to stay under though I also know even the bloated
corpses of the drowned float back into view.

When you do get the knack, I'll watch
from the shallows as you swim away,
leaving barely a ripple in your wake,
each stroke an embrace lifting you to deeper
water where you'll keep your eyes wide

open and sink unseen or swim alone,
holding your breath without my help,
despite my fear and the sting of salt.
Today, you bubble with what you've done,
sneaking up behind me underwater,

laughing that you've tricked me,
swimming back into my arms.

VI.

Running It All Back

Is it just another game the kids like,
weary with home movies of summers
they hardly recall and freckled strangers
whose somersaults, giggles, and squeals

they don't recognize as their own?
I watch myself flip out of the lake
backwards onto the board
like a pilot in trouble ejecting.

The picnic lunch reconstitutes itself.
It's all coming back to me now—
the ball we tossed at the lake that day
flies into my palm, at last the perfect catch,

the keys I fumbled with and dropped
spring into my suddenly magnetized fingers,
ready again to unlock doors
I've begun to ease away from.

We walk backwards toward the car
and back away recklessly toward home.
And I want to run it all back,
past all the sorrow and pain,

harsh words swallowed never to be spoken,
and maybe somewhere we'd be in love again.
I'm beginning to see what chances we take
and what the world will be like without us

when we're gone, the silence in locked houses
where we have not, will never arrive.

Fatigued GI at Lang Vei, 1971

after a photograph by David Burnett

He's sitting on the mud-caked
treads of the shattered Patton tank
it's his mission to repair, reading
the latest missive from home,
back pressed against a capstan,
helmetless, despite the mortars
shredding the air with shrapnel,
maybe a dozen meters away.
His hands and face are smeared
with grease, and he's fastened
his jungle fatigues to the top
like a toddler's cotton pajamas
soaked and soiled by nightmares.
One hand rests lightly on his chin,
and his head's tipped back a little
as if he's pondering the news
he's just received from home.
He looks as tired as a miner
who's aged decades overnight
by his eye-opening descent,
like sleep would be a blessing,
a chance to dig in and forget.
But his eyes reveal the pain
no armor can protect him from—
here's a frazzled boy puzzled
to discover the world is broken
beyond anybody's power to
repair it, not what he expected

or wanted to believe. Can it
ever matter again if the news
from home is good or bad,
who's sick, divorced, or married,
run off and forsaken him?
Even if he should survive,
he knows he can't return
to that quiet town whose lights
he watched recede behind him
in the dark where strangers
laugh and fall in love and marry
and sleep each night unguarded
in one another's arms
as if no one ever has to die.

Night Blindness

You know there's no way back,
retracing one turn at a time
all the wrong turns you've taken,
to that sleepy, sun-bleached street
lined with sycamores and elms,

you remember starting out from,
steering a white Rambler one Sunday,
wide-eyed, believing in the future.
You've traveled many miles since then,
been lost too many times to count,

easing past blind ravines your father
warned you'd plunge into, convinced
you'd never learn from your mistakes.
Every time you checked your mirrors
to see what might be gaining on you

now, you glimpsed your own reflection
and then encroaching darkness.
All the while lonely strangers skidded
toward you out of the mist, the wail
of distant sirens lured you on.

Staring straight ahead, you turned up
the music and ignored the twisted carnage
strewn along the roadside, feeling
oddly responsible. All the wrong turns
you've taken and now begin to call your life

have somehow brought you here to ask
forgiveness of the lost you turned to

in the dark and failed to see, who froze
in the icy glare of your high beams
unable to leap clear in time.

That's why sometimes like tonight,
despite diminished visibility and the chance
of repeating each mistake, you switch
the headlights off and drive on,
speeding deeper into the mystery.

Making Love at the Budget Host Motel

Like water rising in a cistern
seeking its own level,
I wake up sensing trouble
in the dark of 3:00 a.m.
and hear a woman whimpering
beyond the scrim of motel wall.
I listen closely for a moment
before I realize it's the couple
in the next room making love.
Several times I overhear them
rise from wasted passion
into a sweaty furor as they start
and stop and start again,
the wooden bed frame pummeling
the flimsy paneling between us.
He looms over her in darkness,
determined that she'll make it
all the way to him this time.
Out of breath, she lies beneath him,
trying to please her husband
with the only gift he cares about
that she's never had the will to give.
Perhaps the strange surroundings—
being on the road a thousand miles
from home the same way I am—
the freshly laundered linens, scent
of Camay soap, and a few too many
cocktails over dinner have convinced
them somehow this time will be different.
I should stop my ears and turn

away from any scene this sacred,
but I hold my breath and pray for them,
wanting her to make it for us all.
For a moment far from anywhere,
her desperate cries rising to crescendo,
we three are all united as she comes
as close to coming as she ever has before.
Then, without a word from him,
as though it were unmanly to give
utterance to joy, it's over for the moment.
We lie back down in silence,
our separate despairs, our terrible aloneness.
Feeling that I've failed her too,
I fall asleep a second time,
wondering what it is that love requires,
what word or touch that we withhold,
which, if we could freely give it,
might bring us all to ecstasy.

Listening to the Dead
(Birmingham, 1995)

for Randy Blythe

It could be a ghastly scene
straight out of *The Inferno,*
some lower circle of hell glimpsed
through billowing smoke—
the damned in cascading dreadlocks
with lips and nipples pierced
constantly in motion, attempting
to climb higher up the bleachers
or descend to the arena floor below
as though to escape their torment,
the pungent scent of incense,
perspiration, and patchouli
slightly incendiary like brimstone,
except I'm not Italian
and my tour guide isn't Virgil.
As my eyes adjust to the dark,
I see how little's really changed.
These kids could be my children—
hippies, freaks, or Deadheads,
call them what you will, the tribe
I once aspired to be part of,
sounding my adolescent yawp
high on pot in a tie-dyed t-shirt,
my unkempt hair too long for
anybody's parents.
         As if the 1960's
aren't over, an ethereal young woman,

weird and ripe in wire rims, huaraches,
and long tresses, twirls like a dervish
stoned on sinsemilla, and I realize
what enticed me thirty years before
to turn on to the music of the Dead—
that dream of peace, of endless sex,
deep mystery, and *samsara,* of living
without ever having to suffer. Tonight,
in sneakers and light jacket, I'm feeling
awkward, unhip, envying the easy love
everywhere around me, the ecstasy
I sought for years but never quite
discovered.

        When the band slips into
"Easy Wind," J. G. bespectacled
and fat as a kindly math professor,
mingled with the music I hear
the cries of some who haven't made it—
casualties who came to concerts
stoned or drunk not many years ago,
nurturing a dream of ending poverty
and war, racism and hatred, of living
together closer to the earth in harmony
and peace but learned too soon
they'd have to suffer, dragged down
by drugs or drink, by making
a living or pursuing a career, choices
these kids too will have to make.
Knowing the pain ahead might prove
more than can be borne by many
of the dancers on the tarmac down below,

I watch the multi-colored spotlights
swirl in perfect rhythm with the music,
projecting shadows of mandalas
on the unsuspecting crowd, wanting
to believe more tonight than ever
love can somehow change the world.

Not Using My Last Wish

for B. K.

On my first wish,
all the sons you wished for
turned to ravens and flew off.
A twin yourself and a Gemini,
you wanted sets of twins.

I used to grimace at the ritual you kept,
wishing on the first star every night,
as if anything so distant,
whose light had left so many years before
its source might be extinguished,
could guarantee the future.

Half the time you wished
on planets without knowing,
Mars and Venus dividing hope in half;
but still you wouldn't tell me,
though all along I knew,
afraid that if you put it into words,
a world you only dreamed might never be.

Later, we flipped pennies into fountains
and after Sunday dinner scavenged wishbones.
Faithless and blank, I broke them with you,
neither of us seeing in those trivial divisions
how or where our wishes parted,
how our wishes canceled themselves out.

Now the world of second wishes
we endure, made in haste and anger,

wasted, complicates the first.
You wanted marriage,
had two in fact, and children.
I had to make it on my own.
I had to learn to put things into words.

Sometimes at dusk on clear days,
now not even bothering
to guess if it's a planet,
I see the first star rise,
knowing that a third wish
won't undo all this.

But other times near dawn,
reeling over backwards, almost joyful,
I see the double star in Mizar
revolving faintly in the handle of the Dipper,
the attraction between those two
across cold and empty miles of space
buoying them up through the limitless night.

VII.

Epiphany

Nothing is ever enough,
yet sometimes in the afternoon
the green leaves of the Wandering Jew
hanging in the window
grow transparent and hold light.

Then I see the world
I've ached to be a part of
is all a bright reflection,
polished gravel clear as stars.
For a moment I feel

like those Siberian nomads
who believe this world
so much more beautiful
than heaven, the gods
come here to visit in disguise.

Acknowledgments

The author owes a debt of gratitude to the following journals and magazines in which many of the poems in this collection first appeared for their permission to reprint them here.

Appalachian Heritage: "Stroke"
Ascent: "Running It All Back" (awarded the *Ascent* Prize for Poetry)
Birmingham Arts Journal: "Listening to the Dead"
Birmingham Poetry Review: "Enuresis"
Cantilevers: "Via Sacra"
Charlotte Poetry Review: "The Magician's Assistant"
College English: "Invisible Runner," "The Jump Shot"
The Cortland Review: "The Bar in the Lobby of the Peabody Hotel"
Habersham Review: "Poem for Vicki"
Hiram Poetry Review: "Always Stay Calm. Never Shout Fire,"
    "Epiphany," "Those Who Have Vanished"
Louisville Review: "Not Using My Last Wish" (as "Using My
    Last Wish")
The Ohio Journal: "Escape," "The Scream"
The Panhandler: "The Editor of Dreams"
Phase & Cycle: "Extras," "Fatigued GI at Lang Vei, 1971"
Piedmont Literary Review: "Catch"
Plainsongs: "The Counterfeiter's Confession"
POMPA: "The Blue Flames," "Going Home," "Overpass,"
    "Red Giant"
Southern Humanities Review: "Polio"
Southern Poetry Review: "Making Love at the Budget Host Motel"

"Catch" appeared in the anthology *Line Drives: 100 Contemporary Baseball Poems* (Southern Illinois University Press, 2002).

"Making Love at the Budget Host Motel" appeared in the anthology *Don't Leave Hungry: Fifty Years of* Southern Poetry Review (University of Arkansas Press, 2009).

"Running It All Back" appeared in the *Anthology of Magazine Verse & Yearbook of American Poetry* (Monitor Book Co., Inc., 1985).

The author is grateful to the Alabama State Council on the Arts for two Individual Artists Fellowships, which assisted in drafting and revising many of these poems.

I would also like to thank the following individuals who, in one fashion or another, assisted in the completion of these poems: Randy Blythe, David Citino, Brian Conley, Carolyn Elkins, Gordon Grigsby, Ted Haddin, Dick Hague, Jim Mersmann, Jim Quinlivan, Adam Vines, my Thursday poetry workshop at Forest Perk (especially Jerri Beck, who proofread the manuscript), and all the members of the Mermaid Tavern.

Photo of the author by Bill McKinney (bhambilly@gmail.com)

Cover and book design by Diane Kistner (dkistner@futurecycle.org); text type and titling, Adobe Garamond Pro

Cover art: Attrappen (Omega 5) by Paul Klee (1927). This work is in the public domain in the United States because it was first published outside the United States (and not published in the U.S. within 30 days) and it was first published before 1978 without complying with U.S. copyright formalities or after 1978 without copyright notice and it was in the public domain in its home country on the URAA date (January 1, 1996 for most countries).

About FutureCycle Press

FutureCycle Press is dedicated to publishing lasting English-language poetry and flash fiction books, chapbooks, and anthologies in both print-on-demand and ebook formats. Founded in 2007 by long-time independent editor/publishers and partners Diane Kistner and Robert S. King, the press incorporated as a nonprofit in 2012. A number of our editors are distinguished poets and authors in their own right, and we have been actively involved in the small press movement going back to the early seventies.

Our annual anthology, *FutureCycle*, combines poetry and flash fiction. The FutureCycle Poetry Book Prize and honorarium is awarded annually for the best full-length volume of poetry we publish in a calendar year. We are dedicated to giving all authors we publish the care their work deserves, making our catalog of titles the most distinguished it can be, and paying forward any earnings to fund more great books.

We've learned a few things about independent publishing over the years. We've also evolved a unique, resilient publishing model that allows us to focus mainly on vetting and preserving for posterity the most books of exceptional quality without becoming overwhelmed with bookkeeping and mailing, fundraising activities, or taxing editorial and production "bubbles." To find out more about what we are doing, come see us at www.futurecycle.org.

www.ingramcontent.com/pod-product-compliance
Lightning Source LLC
Chambersburg PA
CBHW072359090426
42741CB00012B/3088